...for
these poems
move
all the elephants
into the streets.

Thank-you,

# The Elephants of
# Reckoning

Bob Wiles,

Feb. 8, 1993

# The Elephants of Reckoning

**Indran Amirthanayagam**

HANGING LOOSE PRESS
Brooklyn, New York

Printed in the United States of America
10 9 8 7 6 5 4 3 2 1

Hanging Loose Press thanks the Literature Program of the New York State Council on the Arts and the Fund for Poetry for grants in support of the publication of this book.

Cover art by Greg Decker

Acknowledgments: *Hanging Loose, The Kenyon Review, BOMB, The Portable Lower East Side, The Poetry Project Newsletter, The Indian-American,* and *The Observer. The Island,* and *Channels* in Sri Lanka. Some poems also appeared in *The Open Boat: An Anthology of Poems from Asian America.*

The author wishes to thank the many friends who have served as advisers to these poems, especially Ron Price who examined the galleys, and the MacDowell Colony for a generous grant.

**Library of Congress Cataloging-in-Publication Data**
Amirthanayagam, Indran.
   The elephants of reckoning / Indran Amirthanayagam.
     p.   cm.
   ISBN 0-914610-72-4 (pbk.) — ISBN 0-914610-73-2 (hard) :
   1. Sri Lankans—Poetry. 2. Sri Lanka—Poetry. I. Title.
PR9440.9.A65E4   1992
821—dc20                       92-42368
                                  CIP

 Produced at The Print Center., Inc., 225 Varick St., New York, NY 10014, a non-profit facility for literary and arts-related publications. (212) 206-8465

# Contents

## Outside The Window

The road is dark, and stained with damp grey leaves.
The scissored lightning cuts against the sky.
Now I would accept love's hazard with a sigh
And pass my blind hands gently over her face.

The weather stayed: the impulse cleared,
A stir of the heart, afraid for its loneliness:
The drapes too tattered for the menace which peered
Too frail the window for the waiting darkness.

*—Guy Amirthanayagam*


For the poet Guy Amirthanayagam.
For my mother, Indrani.
For Bob Butman

# The City, with Elephants

# The City, with Elephants

The elephants of reckoning
are bunches of scruff
men and women picking up
thrown out antennae
from the rubbish
bins of the city

to fix on their tubular
bells and horn about
by oil can fires
in the freezing midnight
of the old new year

We ride by their music
every hour in cabs on trains
hearing the pit pat
of our grown-wise pulse
shut in shut out

from the animals
of the dry season
the losers and boozers,
we must not admit our eyes
into the courtyard

the whimsy of chance
and our other excuses—
dollars in pocket—
to write beautiful songs
is all I ask, God

to do right with friends
and love a woman
and live to eighty
have people listen
to the story of my trip to America

The elephants of reckoning
are beaten and hungry
and walk their solitary horrors
out every sunrise slurping
coffee bought with change

while in some houses
freedom-bound lovers
embrace late and read Tagore
about the people working
underneath the falling of empires.

# Words for the Sri Lanka Tourist Office

The King Cobra slides
through our jungles,
and tucked in bushes
by the riverbanks
the grand Kabaragoya
holds court among lizards—

but if you want to swim
at Mount Lavinia, or fly kites
on Galle Face Green, or ride
horse carts in the Jaffna peninsula
of your ancestors, or bear a child
in Colombo General Hospital,

or sleep in Cinnamon Gardens
under a mango tree,
or beg in the Borella Market,
or ride for historical reasons
on patrol boats in the Bay,
or stilt-fish off Matara down South,

just remember here everywhere

there is only man burning
and woman burning

here everywhere

in shallow graves
in deep graves
floating out of salt water
washing down the sands

the dead have tongues
the dead have ears
tongues are speaking to ears

What are they saying?
What are they saying?

Tell us, brown bear
bolting out of your cave.

Tell us, leopard
leaning on your branch.

Tell us, flamingos.
Bend your necks
and pour wine pour wine

Hoopoes, kingfishers,
cranes, have you got your messages
on the bill, are you ready
to sing? Are you going to sing?

Monsoon.

Are you going to sing?

Monsoon.

Are you going to sing?

Monsoon. Monsoon.

# Beating the Drum

The rat still runs
through the tunnels of my blood,
and elephants trumpet
in the war chest of my heart,
and kabaragoyas
the reptile kings
slither out of my eyes.

Beat the drum
beat the drum
facing the Bridge in the fog
facing the towering city
across the water   walking
upon the water
beat the drum.

The fog will clear, the clouds
take back the rain
and the Sun burn again
on the rogue elephant's back
charging up the footpath,

while over the sea
the herd trumpets
while over the sea
the herd trumpets.

# Be Rude, Boy, Again

Shall we take a sea-bath, friend

then burn the salt off
devouring hot prawns

*lying near a fountain*

Shall we swing high
over the palms in Ceylon
cut off a king coconut

snap it on a stone
spoon the sweet flesh
belly in belly out, my friend

*lying near a fountain*

Shall we bathe in arrack
in the evenings singing baila
or act cuckoo in the midday
when all the offices spill

sarongs and shirt-sleeves
sarees and ties
into plantain leaves
housing hot curries

Buggers, you and I
prouder than elephants
rutting in a jungle clearing

fighting cocks   singing
rugger songs   boor boys
in rum shop and shabeen

*flattened near a fountain*

into smooth smooth tile
in a rest area
designed between towers

Come on, machan,
come on, brother,
let's get up
let's get up

The sea is red-flagged
its current murderous
shells in billions
are being thrown up

Let's get up
let's get away
be rude boys
rude boys

drinking toddy
talking politics
jumping ship
jumping ship.

# Biya Kava

The biya kava eat
the water with long beaks,
water crows devouring
fish and eel and rubbish
floating on the lotus pond

the biya kava big and fat
after water   lumber up in air
and gain strength
in the ancient wind
and fly to the mango

they pulp the mango
and pierce the jack
and hundreds gather
in the chief monk's garden
while he rides off

to afternoon prayers
in his Mitsubishi,
accompanied by older Hillmans
and Morris Minors—
the cars of his underlings—

Under the white ant sun
the book disappears
and the boy wipes his sweat
with leftover leaves
and cries as the biya kava

hungry for imaginings
arrow into the eyes
of the boy crying for no useful
reason in the library of ash
and shoot out the back of his head

gnashing their feelers
for critical things
like a boy crying
for no useful reason
or a chief monk

driving a four-wheel
hatchback mini-van
that can hold
six strong thugs
plus the flowers and rice

Biya kava apply
to the word and world
and every living thing
and dead phrase in it said
the Secretary General of Earth

damn you biya kava
eating the Challenger
in front of billions of viewers
damn damn you biya
kava hungry for Amazonian wood

the poem is universal
said the Lord of all
biya kavas at the annual
convention in Honolulu
He said we are blackbird

we are toolshop
we are enlightenment
the renaissance
the chola kingdom
and the Ma ha bha ra ta

We are biya kava
BIYA KAVA
rejoindered the winging
multitudes of delegates
in aloha shirts

and they rose
and flew and ate
the Lord Biya Kava
for their main course
at the closing banquet

to make the whole world
realize that now
there is only
the word
Biya Kava

# There Are Many Things
# I Want To Tell You

There are many things
                    I want to tell you,
how in the lamp night
red candles light your hair,
how in the day, the Sun
like your father kisses
your three-year-old ear,
and your heart and wings flutter,
you spread your arms
in a white gown, a bird
smiles and sleeps in the air,

as you do now,
as you lie before me,
and I take my arms out
into the wind,
and gather sands and trees,
                robins and jasmine;

There are many things
                    I want to tell you,
how I walked in Jaffna town,
arm in arm with you,
and my mother ran from the verandah
out into the street, and my father got
down in a lilac suit from the Austin,
and we met and drank tea,
and read Dickens, and ate mutton—
while the palmyra gave us shade
and Tamil lent us proverbs.

There are many things
                    I want to tell you,
about sun-rich holidays
of morning fish and sea pools,
pianos playing in the drawing room,
lucky holidays where money did not matter,
and I woke up, a terrier
after a deep sleep, and yapped

at mangoes, at jack fruit,
eating like a hog,
a well-mannered fatted hog—
nothing wrong with eating,
said the Roman priest, my teacher,
in the snooze of the afternoon;

There are many things
                              I want to tell you,
how in the churches
the lower castes sat
on the floor, the high
        on benches,

There are many things
we need to do, I want to tell you,
to give every boy and girl
the finest school books
and the loveliest hearts to read
in Tamil, English and Sinhalese,
to help the outcast:
find rice and wood,
a wife or husband,
swim in rainwater pools
for hours, or play cricket,
or live as a hermit
and read the ancient scriptures;

There are many things
                              we could do together,
attend the graduation
of the ten-thousandth woman doctor,
give alms to the crowd
that has met for peace,
a federal agreement
for Ceylon or Lanka,
help arm the revengers
of innocents fix accounts in the Earth,

so the Earth can drive
to the party in Heaven,
in a fine cloak of snow,
a dress of mangoes
for lovemaking,
a cheek slapped, yet strong
like a ten-thousand-year-old oak;

There are many ways
to get ready for the party:
sit in a silent room
and rest your spirit,
fly from land to land,
picking fruits and wines,
pigments to paint boys and girls,
touch your skin
with my skin,
so our skins will melt—

like snow in the Sun,
like blood
when onions trade South
again, or North,
or East, or West,
like a boy
dancing with a girl,
twenty-seven years young
and not seen a dead body yet,

like a man and woman
roped in a pit—
tied in arms and legs,
surrounded by heads
chopped off on platters—

who melt into water,
who steam into the Sun,

like molecules
in the cell of Heaven,
who meet and dance
at The Party of the New.

# The Blood Abroad

When Red Buttons
             was gored
by a rhino in *Hatari*

he bled deep
into my memory

and lives there
with Wayne
giant red roots
out of his arm

Wayne about
to step out
to finish the hunt

and further my lesson
in the primary color of blood

the dragon with long arms
who broomed us
bloody into rooms

the servant boy
who wrapped a rat
in a parcel bow-tied
under his sarong

Granny twisting
a chicken's neck
in her coop

I loved the dripping
of that bird's life

that rich red
vegetable-fed stream
that I longed to drink
as I did Jesus

and lime-green sodas
at Fountain Cafe
after deviled prawns

I walk now
with my blood
    and my devils
through New York streets

while Granny walks even in rain
to the chapel next door
in the early Colombo
morning   to pray

for her children
and grandchildren,
her husband's soul,
their passing to shadow
blood abroad.

# For My Autistic Brother, Chutta

In a room,
a white room,
a small room,

Chutta and Catherine
a young boy and his tutor
a young boy and his master
young knuckles bloody
young teeth knocked soft
          into a cup,
          Catherine's cup.

Her hair, horse's hair
each strand a lash
washed in a pot
dried in the Sun,

a leopard spread
on arms of stone,

the Spirit Leopard
master jungle witch
Catherine clawing
a red breast
tearing a backyard hen,

waits at noon and sniffs
a cub back from school
into a room    Chutta

eyes wide open tweezer held
hanging in a fire, a bulb

Six foot long the knife
loose in a blue gown,
the demon snake skin drum
          drumming      Chutta
          drumming Chutta

crouched    roped

          —thwack, whack—

Chutta    afraid of speech
         still feels and sees
         twenty years later
         still his tongue still.

# The Commissioner of Salt

*Eternity is in love with the productions of time.*
—William Blake

A matter of production goals
and the price of salt
on the commodities exchange

and blue-white gardens
lit by diamond suns
seawater trapped in small ponds
to become salt by the action of the Sun

Trips from the bungalow
out to the flats at first light
to watch over the collection, the tossing

into railway cars, the fresh-painted flats train
pulling the white spice a few hundred yards
to the packing plant, a boy dreaming
in the wondrous blue silence of the morning sea

while men worked, hauling by lorry down South,
loading on to ships, efficiencies of arms and throw weight

and got paid in the administrator's balance
of labor, price and the costs of finding
the most amenable land to harvest

Elephant Pass in the North of Ceylon,

turning the perennial losses of this ministry of salt
to profits drying and ripe in the Sun.

These were among the productions
of my father's time
as the Commissioner of Salt.

# Georgy Uncle

Uncle George, Georgy Uncle, drank a lot at the clubs. He had many arrack and gambling friends, talkers into the night, accompanied by hot prawns and caju nuts, not to mention the several brands of coconut whiskey, arrack distilled at different times, from two-week stabbers to ancient golden caskets, bred and mellowed with fine dust: the golden arrack, a taste which ginger beer or lemonade need not embellish. Arrack mingled with the sheer tongued fire glory of the mixed taste bud, blossoming chilli sweet chutneys on the fresh ocean prawn, born away from cities and breeding farms, still crackling with the primal power whose only adversary is the sack clothed fisherman on stilts, bare arms and legs, blessed head to the rush of sun and wind, not some cloaked scientist examining soil depths in inland fattening and chopping farms.

"Who shall eat the fatted prawn?"

The laughter howled to the stupendous thought like the moaning of hungry wolves on the mountain tops. Who eats the fatted prawn? Spirits scream in the rugby field, darkness surrounding the rugby football club verandah open into midnight, talkers into the night. Who are the wolves moaning into night?

I hear your drunken laugh about the ladies in hostels in the city, girls of other races, ready for fun, students away from village family.

Uncle George drank a lot at the clubs. Otters Swim Club. To swim and drink, to eat hot short eats and have a go at table tennis, or a sweaty shot or two at tennis, and one length of the pool is enough. We're not bloody athletes are we?

It is peaceful by the water side and the children gaily swim races and jump off the diving boards.

## II

Uncle George, Georgy Uncle, brought us Fountain Cafe vanilla ice cream on many glorious occasions. I can hear the happy rumbling of his Volkswagen beetle through the fierce monsoon beating on the windowsill. Over hills and dales, through rivers, I can see his rotund face charging windmills, bearing ice cream.

That ice cream, pure and simple, sweet and succulent, fresh as the new born calf, truly formed just a few hours back. And the commodious green elephant emblemed box in which the gift was carefully placed. Such a delightful treasure hunt, to scrape the box clean, to finish every solid drop and hanging bubble, and then to gaze sadly and beautifully at the empty box, as if some great event that you wished would go on forever must come to an end, and has come to an end.

Georgy Uncle wearing a white shirt, sleeves rolled up, and loose black trousers; slippers and gestures that recall a spirit conductor of small boys' hearts, with deep understanding of their hopes and dreams. And the coronation of the trip to Fountain Cafe where elegant waiters serve boys and uncle in moonlight by the streaming fountain on the cool lawn, bearing the presence of waiters, a few tables and the king's guests.

Those special occasions, trips of the year amongst the dinner guests where uncles and aunts, Pappa and Granny treat the children to a feast.

It is funny to sit on the lawn and stare at the snack bar a hundred feet behind the main restaurant. As children we usually went there for hot dogs and chilli sauce, and merry-go-rounds and plays. But those special trips when we ate with the adult guests, laughed with Uncle George, a full course meal in our stomachs; then we were kings and the world was all right.

Still, the world was always all right when we took a trip in the car and smelt the sauce of the short eat stand.

# III

Uncle George, Georgy Uncle, diabetic, died in 1967, having suffered many months of vomiting and coughing fits. The doorbell rang three times; I exaggerate, I think it was just a knock, and I ran to see who it was. Seven years old in a short sleeved cotton shirt and blue shorts I left the cane chair by the wireless (I wanted to sit as close as I could to the booming machine), and sprinted to the door. My brothers and Renuka, my cousin, were in the living room where the wireless played by the courtyard where Lucky was free to roam. I opened the door and jumped back. Fear and anguish placed their heavy weight on my head and I ran away. My grandmother stood in the eerie light of this fading day. She did not speak, and her face was furrowed by a razor blade. She did not speak, and I saw two tears clinging on each cheek, forever at the mercy of howling winds, away from land, earth and all living things.

Granny, to whom it was such a pleasure to rush along that road between our two houses, under the cover of the large mango trees; Granny who would always give us delicious things to eat.

Granny wore a grey saree and stood at the door for several minutes. To choke up is the correct term; I dashed to the pantry and hid behind it. My fingertips clasping its slightly open door could be seen from the living room. I never told anyone about the shock and the fear and Granny standing several minutes at the door. I remember peeping round the pantry door and watching Granny and Mummy talk in the hallway. Apparently Teasy Aunty had sent Renuka to stay with us for the week so that she could better help Granny overcome her grief.

# Letter from England

*For my grandfather, S. Ratnanather.*

You were a hunter of jungle fowl and birds,
a singer of hymns, odes of whiskey verse.
And you were a king! A regal spirit
on a mountain top washing hands in bowls of gold.

I was eight years old when I went with my father
and mother across the ocean,
far away from your mountain chair,
your confident air.

England was pleasant, rainy and full of cricketers,
and "ministries of silly walks" and Irish terriers.
Remember, you came to our house
bearing "The Pagan Love Song" and "Daisy Daisy".

I was growing up,
I learned you were not only a hunter and king,
but a president of a company as well.
And an old man suffering England's winter. Colds. Pain.

I hear you have had a stroke.
You will not read these words.
I hear you walk about the house
in slippers, talking of Jaffna
and Atchuvelli years.
Your childhood. Palmyra. Jungle fowl.

I hear you get up and walk out of the house
unless somebody catches you at the door,
and you say: "Get away, get away, young man,
I am going to Jaffna on my knees and hands,
with my heart and head. My eyes. My breath."

# Pagan Love Song

'We got a call a few minutes ago. Pappa has died, quietly in
sleep. He received the last rites.'

'Come with me where moonbeams
Light Tahitian skies,
And the starlit waters
Linger in your eyes.

Native hills are calling,
To them we belong,
And we'll cheer each other
With a pagan love song.'

Time is still,
a faint radio sound,
a voice speaks still.

A man has died on an island
far away across many oceans.
Swoosh of a rumbling engine,
an arrow in the eye,
a quivering tree, lightning stone!

'Come in, my son.
Are you going to be a great man?
A great man must write well,
He must command with his pen.'

'Native hills are calling,
To them we belong,
And we'll cheer each other
With a pagan love song.'

Behold!  A man has died on an island
                              Far away across many oceans.

Time is still.
The brain is still.
The bowel is still.
The feet are still.
The spine is still.

Long droning sound, night-sweeping truck
brushes the burnished mind still,
time is still, still
white heat pierces the granite vase,
the mantelpiece clock, the room.

But the grand old man is dead, oh Lord,
the grand old man is dead.
You may try to sing, oh Lord,
but the grand old man is dead.

The grand old man is dead, oh Lord,
the grand old man is dead,
the blades of grass have turned up their heads,
but the grand old man is dead, is dead.

Haunted by shadows,
he drags his feet to a shuffling beat,
out of time, a few scratches on the tile
that sing in the back verandah.

To tread softly in slippers across many rooms,
to tread softly in slippers out of the house
into the blazing Sun.
To crack the gravel on a determined jaunt,
up the street, spectacles heavy on the nose.

Walking past the appearances of things,
lest we see a hole in the ground,
a black tree, and a crow.

Walking past embassies and things,
mini-motorbikes with white shirts
and black trousers screaming for lunch,
betel running red down dark lips.

Come back, come back, whispered the wind.
Come back, come back
said the young man with hand outstretched.
Come back, come back
Premila is waiting in the Dawn.
The palmyra sways in the white Jaffna sun,
Come back, come back
the hawkers are selling roti on Galle Face Green.

Come back, come back, the little boy leads
the hunting trip in the long grass.
'Pappa, the white snake has bitten the mongoose,
the mongoose needs his leaf.'
Come back, come back, come back.

'Come with me where moonbeams
Light Tahitian skies,
And the starlit waters
Linger in your eyes.

Native hills are calling,
To them we belong,
And we'll cheer each other
With a pagan love song.'

# Not Much Art

# I Opened the Screen of Sleep

I opened the screen of sleep
and heard my brother shout,
Hey there, old fellow
how's your game?
All's well over here,
the grass sings in my neck
of the woods,
the field where I bat and bowl
is a carpet cool and warm.

How's your room downstairs,
are you bedded and kicking,
are you eating good food?

I opened the screen of sleep
and heard my brother shout,
I am happy as a fish
in the old county pond,
and every day, rain, sleet or sun
a sweet hot dish
comes smiling down the road,
parks her car and bathes
all delicate in my nooks.

I opened the screen of sleep
and heard no sound,
I called my brother on the phone,
Hey there, old chap, how's your neck
of the woods?
I heard no sound

and thought hard
through the day and night,
how to get out
of my room
and rise up stairs,
how to reach my brother's eyes,
to see with him the field.

I opened the screen of sleep
and found a great abyss,
and a ladder to climb to the sky,

I took the ladder,
eager to roll in the carpet,
eager for the tasty swim—

I knocked on my brother's door,
and knocked and knocked again,
I heard no sound.
I pushed the door in,
and walked about my hands,
until my ears adjusted to the sound
of blood trickling from the fountain,
through the nose and eyes,
the fountain of my brother's head,
in the parlor, quiet and red—

And he said, don't worry, don't be alarmed,
in Heaven we use only the purest blood,
                    to irrigate the field,
                    to make joys bud.

# The Flight of *Boys*

Women protect the men
as *boys*   hidden
in the folds of their sarees

hand-held as baby
brothers in the middle
of the caravan

the more women there are
the safer for the *boys*
as the new-made families

talk to the checkpoint guards
this *boy's* mother
that disappeared's sister

talking   cajoling
we are on a pilgrimage
to the shrine at Kattaragama

our aunt is dying in the capital
we bring her hope
and these small gifts

our bodies
and our spirits
and this *young boy*

clean-shaven shy
thin as bamboo
he's her favorite

he will make her well
please, sir, let us go
let us continue our walk

(on the finest roads
in the whole of Sri Lanka
spanking and fast

to speed armored carriers
and troop convoys
on their journey to the war)

# The Next Holiday of the Moon

When we drove our Land Rover
upon the small roads
and over the wooden bridges
of that lost island

we saw bear in the trees,
leopard leaning in grasses,
huge tuskers and their families
charging across the tracks.

It was a poya day,
the moon's holiday,
or some weekend
when God rested,
and the inhabitants

of the island's cities
journeyed to the mystery,
to the black green leaves
of old and whispering jungles,
slide of a quick snake

under a stone, explosion
of birds off the sanctuary
of river circled
by tall and proud trees.

In that island now,
below the tear of India,
also a tear or pear,
perhaps a state
the size of West Virginia,

there are thousands
of whispering voices
in the cities, afraid
and in wonder, when
will we see the last elephant,

does the snake inherit
the earth, what about
the rat, the beetle?
Don't be silly,
we have napalm, bombers

the size of tuskers,
bombs smaller than butterflies
deadlier than locusts,
come, come, is the army
victorious, are those Tigers

still fighting, who said
'til the last man, why
didn't anybody, anybody
say 'til the last woman
'til the last woman

gave birth
to a child strangled
by some ghost of a doctor
in the delivery room,
some Mengele raging
in what we call

a communal fit
against this strange
and dirty bit of cells
multiplied   dashed
on the orders of Odysseus

on the walls of trees
that built a city
that circle a stream
still bubbling and bleeding
with fish, crocodiles, birds

and words leaping into air
waiting for the next
holiday of the moon.

# Not Much Art

I hear there isn't much art
in the bombing of Jaffna.

Planes fly overhead
and crews pick up
bombs and fling
them down on houses.

On houses, mind you,
no attempt to dig out
guerrillas hiding in bush empires.

No soldier to soldier combat
in the old man on a bicycle
fleeing his burning compound.

I hear from friends
who watch CNN
that a Norwegian crew

made it in and sent
a report for broadcast
in the post-midnight hour,

the scrambly witchy time
when Americans learn
the darknesses of dark lands,

at that hour, even America
is dark watching the Dark Star
attack its sister or father.

How shall the night end,
drummed?   Our eyes punched
                        we sleep.

Versed?        Blindfolded
                        we sleep.

Brush stroked?
              Eyes wide open,
                        we sleep.

There isn't much art
in pill-taking
or the whiskey toothbrush

or 500 laps on one foot
to tire it out    before working
the other foot to tire that out,

when each minute the heart
aches, and lungs draw
cigarettes,   not peace pipes,

when each minute
sons and daughters
raped and murdered

visit the beachhead
of your dreams
bloated and wild-eyed,

and you run
that foot faster
and faster

punch your eyes out
blindfold them
and tear the cloth off,

and in the white dark
fling the balls out
to meet the arriving dreams,

to receive them whole
blood pumped and pumped,
balls soaring
sockets in attendance.

# Teardrop

The teardrop,
the shape
the continents
gave our land

when they split

and made the Bay of Bengal,
put fish in the sea,
and designed the beach

for the landing craft of men
who swing their ropes out
at night, breakfast on fish

and spend their days
hunting villagers for meat and wine,
hunting villagers for televisions,

hunting villagers
to put in the family way
in the family house

plastered clean and whitewashed,
the homes of the friendly hamlet,
Jaffna buoys in the Sun

on the high street, by the well road,
gardens full of mango and jack
and soldiers waving cricket bats.

# The Elephants Are in the Yard

I see the elephants in the yard
Pappa, the white snake too
peering out of the neem tree's trunk
hissing poisons.

Pappa, I see the wild boar
in the thicket, the branches
burning with his smell, Pappa
bring out your gun,

I want to eat the boar's meat
and stare at his head
on my wall, Pappa I see
the elephants in the yard

the partridge and jungle fowl
you shot from the air and bush
to conquer alone
the harvest of the jungle

You were always a sport
took on bird in flight, boar
in fierce charge, your life or his
I see the elephants in the yard

and poachers cockeyed
devouring their tusks in dreams
building grand compounds
massing riches in stainless steel

Pappa, the sport is finished
the elephants are in the yard
and there is no forest
and there are lots of knives

and forks and tractors
and babies to feed
and guerrillas hiding
in the shade of neem and mango

right there beyond the verandah
in the center of the garden
where your dowry will build
your last daughter's house

the elephants spread their heavy bodies
tired from the journey up country
and down country, the long herding,
to some safe peaceful house.

# Upon the Planet

Upon the planet, a spring
green grassland vanished,
a starved animal beaten
become a high and resplendent office

for a biped
who designs a leaf
the giraffe cannot reach,
who makes a sun that breathes
in the blue wind at night

after the fisherman has been extinguished
from the sea, after the toddy tapper
has dropped with a thud
on the cement lot, the burial plot

of the land from where he rose
to climb a sturdy palmyra tree
to suck milk into his pots
give his children milk
and save the rest to buy chillies and meat

after the diamond was discovered
to be hard and colorless
and an intelligent tool
to whittle down the 'Bantu' land
where the African grew so big
('We must dazzle him
and burn him')

after the Tamil guerrillas in small boats
the first craft of the young wood called Eelam,
the boys who left their mothers
by night in silence in fate
to creep by the lanes of Jaffna town
arm in arm, by twos and threes, alone
to run to the boats and training camps,
The Tiger, The Cobra, the young boys

come back to meet the metal whips,
tails lashing bullets, helicopter
gunships flying their mandate
to level the sea,    (and tear the eyes out

of a few 'dirty' boys), uproot the bush
houses, so described in Government House
Order Number 1, the first commandment
of the Presidential decree to destroy all Marxists—

to fish the bush men out
and send the fisher women out
                                        on long boats.

Rape the virgins of the temple

Young soldiers must be allowed.

Brand every man on a bicycle

Young soldiers must be allowed.

Hang mothers upside down to dry,
eliminate the passage of milk.

Kill any children before they feed.

Deny the guerrilla his school.

Bring down to ground the houses
neatly fenced in Jaffna town.

Cut the jack fruit tree
in its garden, husk its thorns.

Prick the pretty young things
milking goats by the garden gates.

Slaughter the goats and wrap
the girls, the sisters of 'The Boys,'
in palmyra leaves dried,
torn from the fences of the houses,
then take them home to the barracks.

Burn the potato and onion
the tobacco, the grape, the plantain fields
in a four o'clock
                    of blood
when the farmer
                    fresh, awake
goes to till his fields
                    in the morning cool.
Make flatter
            the flat land.

Upon the planet, a lake
human-made, green, silver-blue
body-blue, mosquito-green
or yellow, a dump
just over the hill
out of official view.

'What thou lov'st well remains.'

Pull    a screen    around
the lake, the bloated fish
the bodies on the beach.

Pull    down the screen
into a small space.

Crush the space with wine.
Trample the space
with the feet of the man
who turns from the woman
and walks into the sea.

Consecrate the space
with no memorial visits.

Allow the woman
to jump off an aeroplane
and publish no reports
of her apparent suicide.

Then    speak to the children
the old men and women
of the hummingbird and spring trees.

# Eyes Beyond the Border

Eyes beyond the border
cry bullets.

Leafing within the mattress
I found a hair
after many months looking.
It lay still in my hand
like a hand grenade.

Going to Volcanos National Park
I buried the hair under a cactus plant.

Later, I played billiards for money,
dreamt of cancer eating my flesh
and used language like shrapnel.

Injured a few passersby
going to the park
with fruit and wine
to appease the volcano.

Chuttering  sputtering
bullets and grenades
lava flows over fruit
and wine, cactus plant.
To appease or not to appease.

In this house
five miles as the lava flows,
old letters and other memorable fancies,
bangles, breath mints,
screwing in graveyards,
a second hair
under the floorboards.

# Star Over Jaffna

The star will live again,
the painter will take the Night
out again to the films,
and dip blue, dip white.

The fishermen will fix
the holes left by bombs
and ride their boats out
in the bay, and catch
fat prawns under the starry night.

Farmers have begun to plant
tobacco and onions
chillies and brinjals,
weeding out the mines,
the rope burns, the stretched bones

*the soldiers have flown*
*away in aeroplanes.*

Sweet Star, light
pipes and chariots,
garland hundred-armed gods,
put the poet Thiruvaluvar's
head back on the square.

Goon, get thee behind
get thee behind temple walls.

Get thee behind
for one boy and girl
to make handsome children,
trumpets and song.

# Ceylon

The head is cold, the cigarette
cold, the bomb
                    cold,
the wind
the Sun
the white wedding flower
                    cold,

The man who reads the papers,
wrapped in a sheet,
door barred with books
a typewriter, broom
a few cans of fish
a kerosene stove

reads of horses
in flying colors    at Epsom,
of the Queen in her palace
who cries about her common wealth,

so many jewels
so many black bus conductors
so many bits of bus and flesh
near the Fort, the Pettah

where the Tamil shopkeepers
used to make their daily bread,
and build houses in Wellawatte,
now all gone.

In Toronto,
rice and curry
a fist fight,

in Madras
rice and curry
a camp for boys,

grenades and jungle skins
accurate marks man ship
off boats down the barrels
of the Army's gunships.

And the bus on the jungle road
the military checkpoint
the men in uniform, sandals
on their feet, who came to kill

(The sandals was how we could tell
these were terrorists)

No big black boots
marching to the temple
to grab a few young girls
and caress their breasts
and break them down,
"dirty bloody hymens."

No minister with portfolio
at night with soldiers
to hatch the plan   to burn
the Jaffna Public Library

its ola leaf eggs,
its precious historical chicks,
its grand medicinal tapestry
of Ceylon Tamil life served
to wolves, *lion*-hearted men—

> (Pity  the poor lion,
> pity the poor tiger,
> the cobra, the elephant,
> the fish and fowl
> the birds and beasts
> who see their jungle cut down
> to build huts
> for knife throwers   guns
> bombs   rapists
> thieves of every color
>
> who come to drink the milk
> and eat the bread
> of young boys and girls
> who've always been told,
>
> when the beggar comes
> give something, give something you like
>         like your life.)

# The Market Heals

I'm off to market
to buy essences   jet
rat   alley cat   snake
zero   entropy   black hole

and all the white lights
burning in the Sun-whiteness
through the puff pastry
cloud on Spring day

down to Borella Market
for chillies and sprats,
sweet kids of kolikutu plantains,
long tears of mango and jack.

I wish to plant the island
in my Jersey hothouse,
have bread fruit swig
out of the pots, jacaranda

from the Americas
purple in drunken chorus
with Lankan neli crush
splashed in lime-green soda.

I will sing cock a jelly-
fish cockle hooting   rolling
by the sea shore island librettos—

then go downtown
blues market Santiago
to smoke Neruda's poems
and drink Jara's cantatas,

string up a thousand cantos
to unravel the black sun's secrets,
the spells of duende,
the man with the black guitar,

and for good measure
throw in why brown skin
leads to missioning,

then spin my home at the market in Aix
on a Sunday, eating wild boar and grape
listening to the bells ring
the one name of god and man

and at the Union Square
farmer's market
eat Amish goat cheese

polka and beat
my head on the earth
and rise towards Mecca

and hear the jangle
of the bell walking
pot on head for water,

then pinpoint the fixer
to adjust my funny bone
and my sad bone

my tear ducts
my European piano
my long-legged moon walk

my Swedish masseuse
Japanese walking fantasy

my twenty-nine-year body
smoked out of eating hole
public foyer approaching thirty

dying in the conventional way
the new decade the marriage
the lines under my wobbly black ball.

# Kiss

Kissing your lips
I try to forget roses
or the fruit of palmyra trees
sweet and strong

Tongue lolling upon tongue
heart beating
against heart beating,
these are my words
signifying our human bodies
which poetry does not capture,
the absolute desire I have
to kiss your lips
on this hot and sunny afternoon.

I do not know how much longer
I can walk about the garden
kissing roses,

or perambulate the toddy tavern of my dreams
where black faces and white toddy mix
in black and white memories
of Jaffna, Sri Lanka,
my Tamil countrymen
far away on an island across the sea.

Far away and far away
the palmyra fruit and your lips.
To drink toddy now.
To kiss your rosy lips now.
To uproot the roses in my garden
and offer them upon my tongue now.

To fly to Sri Lanka
and grab the last fruit on the tree
before history throws the Tamils into the sea
as is said it will do;

before all this and everything else,
before the apocalypse,
I do so sincerely wish,
though my words may not fit,
to rest my head in your hair
and kiss your lips.

# For M.

I remember the Saturday night
invitation to break bread,
uncork a good French red and dance

the trembling tongues
of our second attempt to sing
to bathe again in our blood

to wet my patched, ancient beard
in the ripe grapes of your scarf

I remember the dream
of meeting at nine p.m.
what more natural thing

than to come by train
from the country, get on the subway
and arrive smiling at your door

to take off my shoes
and hold your hands
and stroke your neck

your apricot ears
your hair of the wheatfield
your eyes of the Trincomalee Sea

all the stars shining
mirroring the night
sky on your face

What more natural thing
than to love you
beyond the dissolving of the moon

the sweeping up of the stars
the ash the ash
the blotting out of the Sun.

# The Animal Heart Breaking

Beyond the re-foresting
of Manhattan

Central Park welcoming cormorants
back to sun, wild ducks to swim the reservoir

(while homeless tumblers
spill on the sidewalk)

elephants are de-tusked in Africa
into bits of herd buried
near tall trees

steaming Asian islands
once saved by typhoons
tiger-toothed sharks
are now bridged to the mainland

spines: beetled, ant-eaten,
become brittling ashen trunks

snakes twisting charmed hips
songbird throats throbbing
in photographs of the mango grove
in Lanka, gone, bled in a pogrom;

on the Earth's burning skin
eyes spill water   make

small clouds of sulphur
on the lava stone suggesting

explosions to come
will always come

the dark god Nature out swaggering
burns a sweet alien thing
into peace beyond crying

(while the band trombones on
and the wizard de-hats
his confettied rabbits
putting galaxies on stage

ta ra rah the music hall
rehearsal in the dog-days
waiting to open
in the Northern Lights

top spinning
off god's thumb, the earth's
spine caterwauling

inside the precise
telescopic eye

of the super skull that feeds
on Everest, withstands
10 on Richter's scale
drinking Martian tsunamis
hot hot winds
for a late night snack)

while in the middle
of the Sea of Tranquility,
the Dead Sea, New York City,
every body of observatory

a paving stone laid down
linking the blood routes
traveling from head to feet
the animal heart
the animal heart  breaking  breaking.

# After the Monsoon

The monsoon broke,
went back to the sea,
and let the children out
to bathe in the day's blood,

lizards wet and dreamy plopping
in puddles, crows mango-beaked
assembling on walls,

Granny out in the pen picking
red eggs while Pappa saronged
in his library leafs through Woolf's

*Village In The Jungle* and *Guide
To The Birds Of Ceylon* by G.M. Henry

Ceylon days, waking up hungry
to bulls-eyes winking, milk tumblered,
running on the road after ball or bird,
spying a rambutan stand, paying a rupee
and eating rambutans,
tearing their spiny skins,
sucking the sweet insides.

Ceylon days, gathering in thousands
every neighborhood marching to the Oval
to see Ceylon defend against England.

Ceylon days, what's left,
I'm trying to gather essences

—a fruit fly feeding
    on the smelling rind
    to tease out that hint of jasmine,
    wedding bud, whiskey tumbling
    at the homecoming party
    over the piano   singing and singing—

trying to secrete essences
from the riverbank, beat
the beet-red saree clean to rouse

a passing goatherd, or a lorry
driver stopping to suck some pan
or just shoot red teeth out
and drink the Sun.

\*

I fold the few stained leaves
of the torn out manuscript
"Ceylon Days"—that sieve dripping
in the alley behind the market, obsessed

with the elephant who charged
our holiday jeep in Yala, that rogue
angry with wheels, hurrays, our traveling songs,
"she's coming round the mountain here she comes"

angry at our leaving the garden
of Eden for jungles beyond the sea

at our fleeing Serendip,
the blood of man and woman spilt,
ashes flung into rivers.

In Eden the rambutan
and mangosteen subsist
for men in cloth and hand grenade.

In Eden boys and girls study
nerves at home, watch television,
or listen to the radio, or sleep, or smoke
ganja while the afternoon rolls into evening.

In Eden the monsoon
has returned to the sea,
and the pen sleeps for a minute.

For a minute, Ceylon has defeated England.

For a minute, rambutans are plentiful
and one rupee will buy a dozen.

For a minute, the elephant ambles
back to his wife and babies.

For a minute, the Sinha lion licks
the Tamil tiger's face on a bed
draped by plantain leaves.

Indran Amirthanayagam, a Sri Lankan Tamil, recognizes his U.S. citizenship with this first book of poems in honor of the elephants that have been left behind in his birthplace. It is a citizenship proud of its roots in such faraway places as Jaffna, London and Honolulu. Amirthanayagam has published poems in *Grand Street, The Kenyon Review, The Massachusetts Review, BOMB, The Literary Review, Night, Hanging Loose* and other magazines. His meditations on plays have appeared in *The Chelsea-Clinton News* and *The Westsider.* He has an M.A. from Columbia University's Graduate School of Journalism and a B.A. from Haverford College. He teaches at Eugene Lang College, The New School, in Manhattan.